Cyber Security & Advanced Persistent Threats (APTs)

Mark Hayward

Published by Mark Hayward, 2025.

Table of Contents

Cyber Security & Advanced Persistent Threats

About

With over 23 years of experience in cyber security, this seasoned professional melds military discipline from their distinguished UK Armed Forces career with deep industry expertise. Their journey into the dynamic realm of cyber security not only transformed their professional life but fuelled a passion for safeguarding digital landscapes. Committed to empowering organizations against evolving threats, they have provided exceptional cyber security services to various government departments. Known for their insightful perspectives and hands-on approach, they make complex concepts accessible and engaging, sharing invaluable knowledge drawn from real-world experience in today's digital age.

Table of Contents

1. Introduction to Cyber Security

2. Understanding Advanced Persistent Threats (APTs)

3. Anatomy of an APT Attack

4. The Kill Chain Model

5. Threat Intelligence in Cyber Security

6. Vulnerability Management

7. Incident Response Planning

8. The Role of Encryption in Cyber Security

1. Introduction to Cyber Security

1.1 Defining Cyber Security

Cyber security is a multifaceted discipline focused on safeguarding sensitive information and critical systems from unauthorized access, theft, damage, or disruption. In today's digital landscape, where data flows freely across interconnected networks, it becomes essential to implement robust security measures. These fundamentals serve as the foundation for all protective strategies, ensuring that the integrity and availability of systems and data remain intact. The evolution of cyber threats necessitates a proactive approach, where understanding vulnerabilities becomes as important as the technologies used to remediate them. It is crucial for cyber security professionals to recognize that their role is not merely reactive, but a continuous effort to stay ahead of malicious actors seeking to exploit weaknesses in both hardware and software.

Key concepts in cyber security include confidentiality, integrity, and availability, often referred to as the CIA triad. Confidentiality ensures that sensitive information is accessible only to those authorized to view it, employing measures such as encryption and access controls to protect data from unauthorized access. Integrity refers to the accuracy and reliability of data; it ensures that information remains unaltered and trustworthy throughout its lifecycle. Techniques such as hashing and digital signatures help maintain integrity by allowing users to verify that data has not been tampered with. Availability ensures that authorized users have reliable access to information and systems when needed, thus preventing issues that can arise from downtime or denial-of-service attacks. Striking a balance among these three principles is pivotal, as a compromise in one can adversely affect the others, highlighting the intricate link between them.

By mastering these foundational concepts, cyber security professionals can better navigate the complexities of the field. Developing a comprehensive security strategy requires an understanding of organizational needs and potential threats. Regular training and awareness programs can empower employees to recognize cyber threats, while automated tools can assist in monitoring and responding to incidents. As threats evolve, so too must the strategies designed to counter them. Staying updated with industry standards and best practices is crucial. Professionals should cultivate a mindset of continuous improvement, where learning and adaptation become integral components of their approach to security.

1.2 The Evolution of Cyber Threats

Cyber threats have undergone significant transformation since their inception in the late 20th century. Initially, the landscape was dominated by simple viruses designed to disrupt computer functionality, such as the Morris Worm in 1988, which unintentionally caused widespread damage. As technology advanced, so did the tactics and motivations behind cyber attacks. The rise of the internet led to new vulnerabilities, with malware evolving into more sophisticated forms like worms and Trojans that could replicate and spread themselves, often with devastating effects. In the early 2000s, the emergence of organized cybercrime introduced ransomware, which demanded payment to regain access to compromised data. This marked a pivotal shift in cyber threats—the focus moved from mere disruption to profit-making. Today, cyber threats include various actors ranging from individual hackers to state-sponsored groups, employing advanced techniques such as phishing, distributed denial-of-service (DDoS) attacks, and advanced persistent threats (APTs) that target specific organizations over extended periods.

The continuous evolution of cyber threats indicates a never-static landscape. As defensive technologies improve, attackers adapt with increased creativity and sophistication. The rise of artificial intelligence and machine learning tools has further accelerated this trend, enabling adversaries to automate attacks and analyze vast amounts of data to identify weaknesses. Additionally, the increasing interconnectivity brought by the Internet of Things (IoT) has expanded the attack surface, as more devices connect to the web and often lack adequate security measures. Recent years have seen a marked increase in supply chain attacks, where hackers infiltrate less secure parts of a business ecosystem to compromise more secure targets. The trend towards remote work has also contributed to the shifting threat landscape, exposing organizations to new risks with employees accessing sensitive data outside traditional office environments. Staying informed about these trends is crucial for cyber security professionals to effectively defend against emergent threats and to foster a resilient security posture.

Monitoring emerging threat vectors and learning from past incidents is essential for staying ahead. Regular training and awareness programs within organizations can help create a proactive culture, making it difficult for cybercriminals to exploit human vulnerabilities. Investing in sophisticated detection and response systems, coupled with a robust incident response plan, will strengthen defenses against the evolving tide of cyber threats.

1.3 The Importance of Cyber Security in Modern Organizations

Cyber security is a critical component for ensuring operational continuity within organizations. As businesses increasingly rely on digital infrastructure for their daily operations, the potential threats posed by cyber incidents become more significant. An effective cyber security strategy helps to safeguard sensitive data, proprietary information, and essential business functions. Without it, organizations risk facing severe disruptions from cyber attacks, such as data breaches, ransomware, and other malicious activities that can cripple essential services. These disruptions not only affect immediate operations but can also lead to long-term financial losses and operational setbacks. In today's interconnected world, maintaining a strong posture against cyber threats is not just a protective measure but a necessity for sustaining business continuity and resilience.

The impact of cyber incidents extends beyond immediate operational disturbances; it significantly influences a company's reputation and the trust its stakeholders place in it. In the aftermath of a cyber attack, customers and partners may question the organization's ability to protect their data, which can erode trust that took years to build. Negative media coverage can amplify these concerns, painting the company as careless or unable to secure its own systems. This loss of reputation can result in decreased customer loyalty, reduced sales, and even legal repercussions. Companies must recognize that a robust cyber security framework is essential not only to defend against threats but also to uphold their reputation in the market. A proactive approach to cyber security fosters a culture of trust, assuring stakeholders that the organization is capable of managing and mitigating risks effectively.

For cyber security professionals, the takeaway is clear: investing in robust cyber security measures is not merely an obligation but a strategic necessity. This includes regular training for employees on best practices to recognize and respond to potential threats, implementing advanced security technologies, and continuously assessing vulnerabilities in the organization's infrastructure. Cyber security should be seen as an integral part of the corporate culture rather than a peripheral concern. By prioritizing cyber security at all levels, organizations can navigate the digital landscape with confidence, protecting their resources while building trust with clients and partners alike.

2. Understanding Advanced Persistent Threats (APTs)

2.1 Definition and Characteristics of APTs

An Advanced Persistent Threat (APT) is typically characterized by its sophisticated nature and the targeted methodology employed by attackers. APTs are not random attacks but are rather orchestrated campaigns that are highly focused on specific individuals, organizations, or sectors. The attackers behind these threats often exhibit significant technical prowess and employ multiple tactics to infiltrate their target. The uniqueness of APTs lies in their combination of stealth, patience, and deliberate strategy. Unlike traditional cyber attacks that may seek immediate gains, APT actors usually aim for long-term access, which enables them to conduct extensive reconnaissance and data collection over time. This prolonged presence often remains undetected for months or even years, allowing attackers to meticulously analyze their targets and execute their objectives without raising alarms.

The long-term nature of APTs is what sets them apart from other forms of cyber threats. Attackers recognize the importance of establishing and maintaining a foothold within the victim's network. This persistence allows them to exfiltrate sensitive data gradually, avoiding detection by blending in with regular network activity. The targeted approach of APTs often involves extensive planning and research about the target's infrastructure, personnel, and vulnerabilities. Cybersecurity professionals must understand that the goal of an APT is not just disruption but rather the extraction of information that can lead to strategic advantages. Effective APT attacks can sometimes lead to the compromise of intellectual property, trade secrets, or even national security, underscoring the critical need for robust defensive measures.

Understanding the dynamics of APTs is essential for cybersecurity professionals tasked with defending against these complex threats. Recognizing that APTs prioritize stealth and longevity means that conventional security measures may not suffice. Organizations must adopt a mindset of continuous monitoring and proactive defense strategies to identify and mitigate these threats. Employing advanced detection mechanisms such as threat intelligence, user behaviour analytics, and regular security assessments can enhance an organization's resilience against APTs. It is also crucial to foster a culture of security awareness, ensuring all employees are alert to potential phishing attempts or unusual activities that could signify a breach. Ultimately, embracing a comprehensive and informed approach to cybersecurity will better equip defenses against the ever-evolving landscape of APTs.

2.2 Historical Context and Notable APT Attacks

Examining the landscape of cyber attacks, several advanced persistent threats (APTs) stand out due to their scale, sophistication, and impact. One notable incident occurred in 2007, targeting Estonia when a series of coordinated attacks crippled its digital infrastructure following political unrest. This incident highlighted the vulnerabilities of a heavily digitized society and marked a significant shift in how nations perceive cyber warfare. Similarly, the 2010 Stuxnet attack, aimed at Iran's nuclear facilities, demonstrated the potential for cyber weapons to achieve geopolitical goals. As these attacks unfolded, they ushered in discussions about national cyber defenses and the importance of cooperation among nations to address cyber threats. The repercussions of these events resonate today and continue to inform how organizations approach cybersecurity.

Key players in these APT operations typically include state-sponsored hackers and organized cybercrime groups, each motivated by distinct objectives. Nation-states often engage in cyber espionage to gain intelligence, disrupt operations, or establish dominance over rivals, with groups like APT28 (Fancy Bear) and APT29 (Cozy Bear) representing Russian interests. Meanwhile, Chinese groups, like APT10, have been known to target industry secrets and sensitive data to bolster their technological advancements. Understanding the motivations behind these attacks, whether for national security, economic gain, or ideological reasons, is essential for preparing effective defenses. Cybersecurity professionals must acknowledge the complexity of these actors and their relentless pursuit of strategic advantages to devise robust protection mechanisms.

Sharing information about notable APTs is crucial for cyber defense. Cybersecurity teams should conduct regular threat assessments, stay updated on emerging vulnerabilities, and engage in information-sharing initiatives with industry peers. This collaborative approach not only enhances situational awareness but also empowers organizations to adopt proactive strategies against potential attacks.

2.3 How APTs Differ from Other Cyber Threats

Advanced Persistent Threats (APTs) stand in stark contrast to traditional cyber threats such as malware and phishing. While malware is often indiscriminate, targeting a wide range of systems to exploit vulnerabilities, APTs are highly targeted and calculated in their approach. Malware can be deployed en masse through malicious downloads or spam emails, resulting in a quick gain for the attacker. In contrast, an APT involves an ongoing effort, where the attacker seeks to infiltrate a specific organization and maintain a foothold over time. Phishing attacks, similarly, aim to deceive individuals into divulging sensitive information. However, APTs utilize a series of sophisticated social engineering techniques that are tailored to the specific environment of the victim organization. This leads to a deeper and more strategic breach rather than the immediate but fleeting gains seen in typical phishing schemes.

What sets APTs apart from other cyber threats are their strategic objectives and the methods employed to achieve them. APT attackers often have clearly defined goals, such as stealing intellectual property, compromising sensitive data, or even disrupting critical infrastructure. They employ a range of tactics, such as reconnaissance, where they gather intelligence about their target over an extended period. The methodology often involves exploiting weak points in an organization's security posture, which may include targeting employees through spear phishing, planting malware that establishes backdoors, and moving laterally within networks once a foothold is gained. This careful orchestration allows attackers to maintain long-term access to the target's systems, making detection and removal significantly more challenging. APTs can adapt and change tactics, reflecting the security measures employed by organizations, which is a notable difference from conventional cyber threats that often follow consistent patterns and methodologies.

Understanding the nuances and complexities of APTs is vital for cyber security professionals. With their strategic nature and targeted approach, APTs require a multi-layered defense strategy that not only focuses on traditional measures but also incorporates advanced detection systems, employee training to recognize tailored social engineering attempts, and continuous monitoring for unusual activities within the network. Implementing threat intelligence that is actionable and up-to-date can also be invaluable in anticipating and mitigating threats before they escalate into significant breaches.

3. Anatomy of an APT Attack

3.1 Reconnaissance Phase Overview

The reconnaissance phase is a critical initial step in preparing for an advanced persistent threat (APT) attack. During this phase, attackers actively gather information about their target to identify vulnerabilities that can be exploited later. This stage is all about creating a comprehensive profile of the target, which can include understanding the organization's infrastructure, employees, technologies, and overall security posture. Intelligence collected during this phase is often the foundation upon which the remainder of the attack is built. Successful reconnaissance enables attackers to tailor their strategies, making their approaches more effective and less detectable.

Various techniques are employed for intelligence gathering on targets, each varying in complexity and depth. Common methods include open-source intelligence (OSINT), where attackers scour public information such as social media profiles, websites, and forums to gather data. They might also engage in social engineering, attempting to manipulate individuals within the target organization to divulge sensitive information. Scanning and probing tools are frequently used to map network structures and identify exposed services. More sophisticated attackers might deploy advanced techniques such as spear phishing, where they send targeted emails designed to deceive specific employees into revealing crucial details. These intelligence-gathering methods create a detailed map of the target's environment, which significantly increases the likelihood of a successful penetration later in the attack sequence.

Understanding the reconnaissance phase enables cyber security professionals to anticipate and mitigate potential threats. Having established procedures in place to scrutinize anomalies in network traffic and monitor social media activity related to the organization can prove invaluable. Implementing a strong security awareness program that educates employees on the risks of social engineering can also help in reducing the surface area for attackers. By remaining one step ahead during this preparatory phase, organizations can fortify their defenses against the more invasive efforts that follow.

3.2 Initial Compromise Tactics

Understanding how attackers gain initial access to their targets is crucial for cybersecurity professionals tasked with safeguarding their organizations. Initial compromise methods can vary widely, yet they often share common themes that can be analyzed to enhance defensive measures. One prevalent method is the use of phishing, where attackers craft convincing emails to trick victims into providing sensitive information or clicking on malicious links. This technique relies on social engineering to exploit human psychology, making it essential for organizations to conduct regular training on recognizing potential threats.

Another technique commonly employed is exploiting vulnerabilities in software or systems. Cybercriminals often scan for outdated software applications with known vulnerabilities, allowing them to execute code remotely and take control of a system. Consequently, maintaining an up-to-date inventory of all software, along with timely patch management, is essential in reducing the attack surface. Additionally, attackers might utilize tools such as Metasploit to automate the discovery and exploitation of these vulnerabilities, highlighting the importance of rigorous security audits and applying the principle of least privilege.

Several case studies showcase typical initial compromise techniques that underline their effectiveness. For instance, the 2016 Democratic National Committee email breach exemplifies phishing's devastating potential. Attackers sent emails disguised as Google security alerts, prompting employees to change their passwords. Once an employee fell for this deception, attackers gained access to sensitive information, leading to substantial political repercussions. Another notable example is the WannaCry ransomware attack, which exploited the EternalBlue vulnerability within Windows systems. By targeting organizations that failed to apply available patches, the attackers gained access to numerous systems worldwide, causing chaos and financial loss. Observing these incidents underscores the importance of employee awareness and comprehensive patch management strategies to mitigate similar threats in the future.

Effectively addressing initial compromise tactics involves a proactive approach that encompasses both technology and human factors. Regularly updated training programs focused on recognizing phishing attempts, coupled with robust security measures such as two-factor authentication, can significantly disrupt an attacker's ability to gain unauthorized access. Understanding and adapting to these initial compromise tactics is not just a defensive necessity, but a critical aspect of cultivating a resilient cybersecurity posture.

3.3 Command and Control Mechanisms

Understanding how attackers establish and maintain communication with compromised systems is critical in cybersecurity. Attackers often leverage command and control (C2) mechanisms to facilitate this communication, which allows them to send instructions to infected devices and retrieve stolen data. These communication channels can take various forms, including HTTP requests, peer-to-peer networks, or even using social media platforms. The choice of a channel is influenced by the need to evade detection by security tools, which often monitor traditional protocols more stringently. Secure protocols like HTTPS or encrypted payloads further obfuscate communication, making it challenging for defenders to decipher the attacker's intent. Additionally, attackers may employ techniques such as domain generation algorithms (DGA) to dynamically create a list of domains to use for C2, decreasing the likelihood that a single domain will be blacklisted. This adaptability in establishing and maintaining connection underscores the sophisticated nature of contemporary cyber threats.

An overview of common C2 frameworks used in advanced persistent threat (APT) operations reveals the arsenal at attackers' disposal. Frameworks such as Cobalt Strike, Metasploit, and Empire provide attackers with user-friendly interfaces and a rich set of tools for managing compromised systems. Cobalt Strike, for instance, mimics legitimate security testing tools, which can further obfuscate malicious activities. Its capabilities, including the use of beacons for communication with compromised systems, allow attackers to deploy payloads and execute commands remotely. Other frameworks like Metasploit facilitate the exploitation of vulnerabilities and post-exploitation activities, while Empire specializes in PowerShell-based attacks that can operate stealthily within Windows environments. Understanding these frameworks enables cybersecurity professionals to better prepare and detect the signatures and behaviours associated with malicious activities, leading to more robust defenses against APT events.

The effectiveness of C2 mechanisms can often be diminished by the proactive monitoring and response protocols employed by organizations. Ensuring thorough logging of all network traffic and using anomaly detection tools can aid in identifying unusual patterns that signify potential C2 communications. Moreover, implementing least privilege principles and segmenting networks can limit attackers' lateral movement, making it more difficult for them to establish and maintain their command infrastructure. Integrating threat intelligence feeds can also provide context on emerging C2 tactics and techniques, allowing organizations to stay ahead of potential threats. By fostering a culture of vigilance and preparedness, cybersecurity teams can significantly reduce the effectiveness of command and control mechanisms used by attackers.

4. The Kill Chain Model

4.1 Stages of the Kill Chain Explained

The kill chain model, originally developed for military planning, comprises several phases that outline the process of a cyber attack. Each stage plays a crucial role in understanding how adversaries operate, particularly in advanced persistent threats (APTs). The stages typically include reconnaissance, weaponization, delivery, exploitation, installation, command and control, and actions on objectives. In the reconnaissance phase, attackers gather information about the target, leveraging open-source intelligence and network mapping to identify vulnerabilities. Weaponization then follows, where the attacker creates a malicious payload tailored to exploit the identified weakness. Delivery involves sending the weaponized payload through various means, such as phishing emails or web applications. Exploitation occurs when the malicious payload is executed, granting the attacker a foothold within the environment. After exploitation, the installation phase allows the attacker to establish persistence through creating backdoors or other hidden access points. Command and control enables the attacker to interact remotely with the compromised systems, facilitating further actions. Lastly, actions on objectives refer to the operational goals of the attacker, which may involve data theft, system disruption, or espionage.

The kill chain model is instrumental in comprehending the lifecycle of an attack, enabling cybersecurity professionals to identify and mitigate risks at each stage. By understanding how each phase unfolds, defenders can implement targeted strategies to disrupt the attack cycle. For instance, efforts tied to reconnaissance might include enhancing threat intelligence and user awareness training to diminish the effectiveness of initial data gathering. Likewise, implementing robust email filtering can help in intercepting weaponization and delivery attempts. Recognizing the significance of each stage allows for a more sophisticated defensive posture. Responding to the installation of malware can be approached by employing endpoint protection solutions and ensuring timely system updates. The model also emphasizes the need for an integrated approach, urging teams to collaborate across different security domains to address the complexity of modern threats. By dissecting the kill chain, organizations are better equipped to predict adversarial behaviour and fortify their defenses.

Understanding the kill chain facilitates a proactive defense rather than a reactive one. This awareness is critical as it empowers teams not just to respond to breaches but to anticipate and prevent them. One practical tip is to conduct regular simulations that mimic attack scenarios based on the kill chain to test and evaluate your organization's security measures. By practicing responses at each stage, teams can refine their strategies, strengthen their procedures, and reduce the window of opportunity for attackers.

4.2 Applying the Kill Chain to APT Defense

The kill chain framework, originally developed by Lockheed Martin, offers a structured approach to understanding and countering advanced persistent threats (APTs). To effectively leverage this framework, organizations should focus on integrating it into their existing security protocols. This involves aligning detection mechanisms with each stage of the kill chain, which can significantly enhance overall defense capabilities. For instance, improving initial reconnaissance detection could aid in identifying potential breaches before they materialize. Additionally, organizations should invest in threat intelligence that correlates with different stages of the kill chain to refine their predictive analytics. By doing so, security teams can not only respond to incidents more quickly but can also pre-emptively close gaps in their defenses, thus creating a more resilient security posture.

Monitoring APT activities at various stages of the kill chain is critical for disruption and mitigation. Focusing on each phase—from initial reconnaissance to delivery, exploitation, installation, command and control, and action on objectives—allows security professionals to identify anomalies that may indicate malicious intent. For instance, in the delivery phase, monitoring for unusual email patterns or downloading behaviours can prevent the execution of payloads that exploit vulnerabilities. Leveraging automated tools and analytics can enhance the detection of these threats; implementing user behaviour analytics (UBA) can provide insights into deviations from normal activity, signalling a potential breach. Moreover, ongoing monitoring should involve continuous learning and adaptation of detection mechanisms, as threat actors are always refining their tactics.

Practical measures, such as employing decoy systems and honeypots at various stages, can further complicate an adversary's efforts. These tactics not only capture the attention of intruders but also provide invaluable data for understanding attacker behaviours and methodologies. Continuous improvement in incident response and threat hunting capabilities should be the goal, ensuring that organizations remain several steps ahead of their adversaries. Cybersecurity professionals must actively review and adjust their strategies to stay one step ahead of APT actors while fostering a culture of security awareness throughout the organization.

4.3 Case Studies of Kill Chain in Real Scenarios

In the realm of advanced persistent threats (APTs), understanding the kill chain framework has proven vital in dissecting cyber incidents. A notable example is the attack on Target in 2013. Attackers infiltrated Target's network through compromised vendor credentials. They executed the initial reconnaissance phase, identifying weak spots, which enabled them to move laterally within Target's infrastructure. Once inside, they deployed malware designed to harvest credit card information, effectively advancing through the kill chain stages: delivery, exploitation, installation, command and control, and action on objectives. The breach led to the exposure of millions of credit card accounts, highlighting the critical need for organizations to bolster their defenses at each stage of the kill chain.

Another illustrative incident occurred with the SolarWinds cyberattack in 2020. Attackers used supply chain compromises to distribute malicious code through legitimate updates, manipulating the reconnaissance and delivery phases. The complexity was heightened as the malware facilitated further exploitation within victim networks, ultimately enabling actors to access sensitive information from multiple government and private sector organizations. This case underscores the importance of monitoring not only the internal network but also third-party vendors, as they can introduce vulnerabilities that attackers can exploit.

Analyzing the Target and SolarWinds incidents reveals several crucial lessons for organizations aiming to fortify their cybersecurity posture. One significant takeaway is the importance of a multi-layered defense strategy that includes stringent vendor management protocols. Organizations must recognize that their security is only as strong as their weakest link. By implementing severe access controls, strong authentication measures, and continuous monitoring, businesses can effectively disrupt the kill chain, especially during the early phases where attackers are attempting to gain entry.

Another lesson is the necessity of comprehensive employee training and awareness programs. Humans often represent the most vulnerable aspect of cybersecurity. Ensuring personnel can recognize phishing attempts and suspicious activity is essential in reducing the risk of exploitation during the reconnaissance and delivery stages. Additionally, integrating threat intelligence into an organization's security framework allows for proactive identification of potential threats, allowing for a quicker response and mitigation of risks before they escalate into significant breaches. These insights highlight that cybersecurity is not solely a technological challenge; it demands organizational commitment, continuous vigilance, and an adaptive mindset to stay ahead of evolving threats.

As organizations continue to grapple with the sophisticated tactics employed by APT groups, employing the kill chain model serves as a foundational tool for analyzing and enhancing defensive strategies. Strengthening the various stages of the kill chain, particularly through proactive threat monitoring and employee education, can significantly reduce vulnerability and enhance incident response effectiveness. Establishing ongoing training and reinforcement strategies for staff can create a security-conscious culture, further fortifying defenses.

5. Threat Intelligence in Cyber Security

5.1 Collection and Analysis of Threat Data

Effective collection of threat intelligence starts with a systematic approach. Cybersecurity professionals can use a combination of automated tools and manual processes to gather relevant data from a variety of sources. These sources can include open-source intelligence (OSINT), vendor-provided information, internal logs, and threat-sharing platforms. Utilizing tools like Security Information and Event Management (SIEM) systems can enhance the collection process by providing centralized logging and real-time analysis of security events. It's also essential to establish relationships with information-sharing organizations, as they can provide valuable insights into emerging threats. By prioritizing the relevance and reliability of the collected data, professionals can ensure that the threat intelligence gleaned is both actionable and timely.

Once data is collected, the next crucial step is analysis. Cybersecurity experts need to employ a variety of techniques to sift through the information and derive meaningful insights. Techniques such as pattern recognition and data mining can help identify suspicious behaviour and trends indicative of potential attacks. Advanced analytics, including machine learning algorithms, can significantly enhance the capability to detect anomalies in network traffic or user behaviour. Furthermore, leveraging threat models allows professionals to assess risks in a structured manner, guiding decision-making processes effectively. Combining quantitative analysis with qualitative assessments ensures that the insights drawn are comprehensive, supporting proactive threat mitigation strategies.

One practical tip for enhancing the process of threat intelligence collection and analysis is to establish a feedback loop. By continuously refining data sources and analytical techniques based on the outcomes of past decisions, professionals can build a more robust threat intelligence framework. This iterative approach not only strengthens the organization's defenses but also fosters a culture of learning and adaptation in the face of evolving cyber threats.

5.2 Threat Intelligence Sharing Platforms

Threat intelligence sharing platforms are specialized tools and networks that facilitate the exchange of information regarding cybersecurity threats among organizations. These platforms enable entities to collaborate in recognizing and mitigating potential risks by pooling information about malicious activities, indicators of compromise (IOCs), vulnerabilities, and tactics employed by threat actors. By centralizing this information, organizations can enhance their situational awareness and build a more robust defense posture. Noteworthy platforms include the Information Sharing and Analysis Centers (ISACs), which are sector-specific networks, and commercial solutions that offer real-time threat data, analytics, and community sharing features. These platforms streamline the process of collecting, processing, and disseminating threat intelligence, making it accessible for timely decision-making in response to evolving cyber threats.

The importance of collaborative intelligence-sharing amid organizations cannot be overstated. By participating in these platforms, companies can benefit from a more comprehensive understanding of the threat landscape. Shared intelligence can lead to quicker responses to incidents, as organizations are better informed about emerging threats and common attack vectors. Furthermore, by collaborating, entities can improve their overall cybersecurity maturity. This collective effort not only bolsters an individual organization's defenses but also creates a stronger overall security ecosystem, where threats are recognized and neutralized more effectively. The insights gained through shared intelligence help organizations make informed security investments and prioritize their resources based on a clearer understanding of prevalent threats in their sector.

To maximize the benefits of threat intelligence sharing platforms, organizations should actively engage in contributing their own insights while also utilizing the shared information. Establishing trust among peers and ensuring the anonymity of shared data can enable a more open exchange. Organizations should also evaluate the platforms regularly to ensure they are leveraging the most relevant and effective mechanisms for information sharing. A proactive approach to threat intelligence sharing can significantly enhance an organization's cybersecurity posture and resilience against attacks.

5.3 Significance of Real-Time Threat Intelligence

The critical role of real-time data in proactive cyber defense cannot be overstated. In today's digital landscape, threats evolve rapidly, and organizations must adapt just as quickly. Real-time threat intelligence provides timely insights into emerging threats, enabling security teams to take proactive measures rather than reactive ones. With this type of data, cybersecurity professionals can identify potential vulnerabilities in their systems before they are exploited. For example, when a new malware variant is detected, real-time intelligence helps prioritize which systems need immediate patches and gives teams the information they need to defend against the latest tactics used by cybercriminals. By integrating real-time data into their security operations, organizations can significantly reduce their reaction time to threats, effectively minimizing the potential damage from cyberattacks.

Discussion of case studies highlights the impact of timely intelligence on mitigating threats. One notable case involved a major financial institution that faced an increasing number of phishing attempts. By implementing a real-time threat intelligence platform, the organization was able to receive immediate alerts about new phishing schemes and the indicators of compromise associated with them. Within days, the security team identified and blocked multiple attempted breaches, safeguarding sensitive client information. Another case study focused on a healthcare provider that successfully thwarted a ransomware attack through proactive monitoring of dark web forums where such threats were discussed. By leveraging real-time updates on ransomware trends, the organization not only protected their data but also enhanced their incident response strategy. These examples underscore the effectiveness of utilizing real-time intelligence, demonstrating that timely information is not merely an advantage but a necessity in the evolving landscape of cybersecurity.

Incorporating real-time threat intelligence into daily operations allows security professionals to stay a step ahead of attackers. Ensuring that teams are equipped with the latest intelligence not only enhances their defensive capabilities but also transforms their cybersecurity posture into one that anticipates rather than merely reacts. To maximize the benefits of real-time data, organizations should establish clear communication channels among their security teams and ensure that intelligence services are regularly updated and integrated into existing workflows.

6. Vulnerability Management

6.1 Identifying and Assessing Vulnerabilities

Comprehensive methods for systematic identification of IT vulnerabilities encompass various strategies that integrate both automated and manual processes. Effective vulnerability identification starts with a thorough inventory of the IT assets within an organization. Knowing what components are in play, including hardware, software, and networks, provides a critical foundation for vulnerability assessment. Tools such as vulnerability scanners can be employed to automatically detect known vulnerabilities in systems by cross-referencing them against databases of security flaws. Additionally, penetration testing, which involves simulating attacks on the network to uncover weaknesses, serves as a proactive approach to identification. Moreover, collecting threat intelligence and keeping abreast of the latest security advisories can further enhance the identification process. Engaging in regular audits and employing a framework like the MITRE ATT&CK or OWASP Top Ten can systematically guide professionals in identifying vulnerabilities in a structured manner.

Techniques for assessing the severity and impact of identified vulnerabilities require a combination of qualitative and quantitative approaches. The Common Vulnerability Scoring System (CVSS) is widely used for assigning severity scores to vulnerabilities, taking into account factors such as exploitability, the potential impact on confidentiality, integrity, and availability. Assessing the context in which a vulnerability exists is equally important, as the impact can vary significantly based on the organization's specific environment and threat landscape. Utilizing risk assessment methodologies, such as qualitative risk assessments that judge the significance of vulnerabilities based on their potential consequences, can be paired with quantitative measures that include estimating the potential financial impact of an exploit. This holistic approach enables cyber security professionals to prioritize vulnerabilities effectively, focusing resources on those that pose the greatest risk.

When conducting vulnerability assessments, it is crucial to adopt an iterative strategy that allows for continuous monitoring and responsiveness to new threats. Maintaining an updated risk register and regularly revisiting the assessment process ensures that organizations can adapt to the evolving cyber threat landscape. One practical tip is to embed vulnerability management within a broader security program, integrating tools and processes that promote collaboration across IT and security teams. This fosters a culture of shared responsibility and strengthens the overall security posture of the organization.

6.2 Patch Management Strategies

Implementing an effective patch management program requires a structured approach that focuses on best practices tailored to meet the specific needs of an organization. It begins with the establishment of a clear policy that outlines responsibilities, processes, and timelines for patch deployment. Regularly assessing the patch management process and continuously improving it based on feedback and evolving best practices ensures relevance in a rapidly changing cyber landscape. Organizations should maintain an inventory of all hardware and software assets, as understanding what needs to be patched is the first step in the process. Automated tools can significantly enhance efficiency by regularly scanning for missing patches and automating the deployment process. However, organizations must also consider the specific context of their environment, as not all patches are equally critical. Testing patches in a controlled environment before wide deployment can help prevent unintended disruptions and ensure compatibility with existing systems. Clear communication about updates and potential impacts to users reinforces the importance of the patch management strategy and fosters a culture of awareness around cybersecurity. Additionally, regularly scheduling maintenance windows allows IT teams to apply patches with minimal disruption to business operations.

Prioritizing patches based on vulnerability assessments is essential for optimizing patch management efforts. Cybersecurity professionals should conduct regular vulnerability scans to identify known vulnerabilities in their systems and evaluate the severity of each. Utilizing frameworks like the Common Vulnerability Scoring System (CVSS) can aid in determining the urgency of applying patches. High-severity vulnerabilities pose significant risks and should be addressed as soon as they are identified. In contrast, lower-severity issues may be scheduled for later deployment, allowing teams to allocate resources efficiently. It's important to focus not only on the vulnerabilities themselves but also on potential exploitability. If a vulnerability is being actively exploited in the wild, it should be treated with a higher priority regardless of its CVSS score. Furthermore, organizations should consider the specific context of their business and the data they manage, as critical systems will require a more immediate response. Continuous monitoring and threat intelligence can also inform prioritization, enabling organizations to stay ahead of emerging vulnerabilities and ensure that critical fixes are applied promptly and effectively.

A proactive approach to patch management integrates ongoing education and training for cybersecurity teams. Familiarity with the tools, techniques, and risk factors involved in the patching process enhances the team's ability to respond promptly and effectively to new vulnerabilities. Regularly reviewing the patch management process and analyzing its effectiveness can lead to smarter patch deployment strategies. Keeping abreast of vendor notifications and cybersecurity advisories also plays a critical role in maintaining a robust patch management program. By staying informed, organizations can be prepared to respond quickly to emerging threats. As a practical tip, consider implementing a risk-based decision-making framework, allowing teams to weigh the potential impact of unpatched vulnerabilities against the operational risks associated with patching. This tailored approach can help balance security needs with business objectives.

6.3 Role of Vulnerability Scanning Tools

Common vulnerability scanning tools are essential in the landscape of cybersecurity, functioning as the frontline defenders that help identify potential weaknesses within an organization's network and systems. Tools like Nessus, Qualys, and Rapid7's InsightVM are widely recognized in the industry. Nessus offers comprehensive scanning capabilities and is appreciated for its extensive plugin library that addresses various vulnerabilities. Qualys, on the other hand, provides cloud-based solutions that simplify deployment and management while delivering real-time insights. Rapid7's InsightVM emphasizes continuous monitoring with live dashboards that empower organizations to prioritize vulnerabilities based on risk. Each tool has its unique strengths, but they share the commonality of automating the vulnerability management process, making it less cumbersome and more proactive.

Integrating vulnerability scanning tools into an organization's security framework is pivotal for enhancing overall security posture. These tools should not act in isolation; rather, they need to seamlessly blend with existing security measures such as firewalls, intrusion detection systems, and security information and event management (SIEM) solutions. Successful integration involves not just deploying the tools, but also establishing processes for regular scanning and analysis of the results. Organizations should develop a robust vulnerability management policy that outlines how and when scans will be performed, how findings will be prioritized, and the steps for remediation. Ensuring that the scanning tools are aligned with the organization's risk management strategies can greatly enhance incident response times and reduce overall exposure to attacks.

To maximize the benefits of vulnerability scanning tools, it's vital to foster a culture of security awareness within the organization. This includes training team members not only on how to use the tools effectively but also on the importance of addressing vulnerabilities promptly. Establishing a feedback loop, where results from the scanning tools inform the broader security strategy and policy updates, creates a dynamic approach to security management. Furthermore, regularly revisiting the choice of tools and their configuration in the context of evolving threats will ensure that the organization remains resilient and responsive in an increasingly complex cybersecurity landscape. Always remember that vulnerability scanning is not a one-time event; it's a continuous commitment to maintaining a secure environment that necessitates diligence and proactive engagement.

7. Incident Response Planning

7.1 Developing an Incident Response Plan

When formulating an incident response plan, several key components are essential to ensure its effectiveness. First, clearly define the roles and responsibilities of each team member involved in the response process. This clarity will help facilitate quick decision-making during crises. Additionally, an inventory of resources, such as tools, technologies, and personnel, must be created, so all necessary elements are readily available. It's vital to develop a communication plan to guide internal and external communications during an incident, maintaining transparency while protecting sensitive information. Regular training and simulations can significantly enhance the preparedness of the team. The plan should also include post-incident review procedures to analyze actions taken and derive lessons learned for future improvements.

Aligning incident response plans with business objectives is crucial to maintaining organizational stability and resilience. An effective incident response plan isn't just a technical document; it should reflect the broader goals of the organization. When the response strategies are woven into the fabric of business objectives, the organization can better mitigate risks that directly impact its mission and reputation. Establishing clear benchmarks to measure the success of incident response activities ensures that these measures support the organization's priorities. Moreover, engaging stakeholders from different business units can help promote a culture of cybersecurity awareness throughout the organization, ensuring that everyone understands their role in the incident response process.

A practical tip for cyber security professionals is to regularly review and test the incident response plan against evolving threats and changing business landscapes. The digital landscape is continuously evolving, and so are the tactics employed by cyber adversaries. By staying proactive and adaptable, an organization can strengthen its incident response capabilities and ensure it is prepared for any eventuality.

7.2 Incident Response Team Structure

Defining roles and responsibilities within an incident response team is crucial for its effectiveness. Each member should have a clear understanding of their specific duties, which typically range from technical analysis to communication with stakeholders. Common roles include the Incident Response Manager, who oversees the entire response process, ensuring that team members effectively coordinate their efforts. Technical specialists are responsible for identifying the nature and source of the incident. They may include forensic analysts, who provide insights into how the breach occurred, and IT personnel, who work on containing and mitigating the threat. Additionally, communication roles are pivotal; they ensure that relevant information is disseminated to organizational leaders and external parties as necessary. By establishing these distinct roles, organizations ensure that each aspect of the incident response is handled by qualified professionals, reducing confusion and improving response times during a crisis.

An overview of effective team dynamics and communication protocols further enhances incident response. Clear communication channels need to be established to facilitate the rapid sharing of information, especially during high-pressure situations. Regular team meetings should be conducted to review procedures and roles, fostering a culture of collaboration and preparedness. Utilizing incident management tools can streamline communication and provide real-time updates, allowing all team members to stay informed. Moreover, it is essential to develop an environment where team members feel comfortable sharing their observations and suggestions, as this can lead to innovative solutions and improvements in response strategies. Encouraging open communication fosters trust and ensures that every team member is engaged and understands the collective mission during an incident. These dynamics, combined with well-outlined protocols, can significantly impact a team's performance, enabling them to respond effectively to complex cyber threats.

Regular training and simulations should be incorporated into the team's routine to solidify these structures and practices. Engaging in practical exercises not only reinforces the defined roles and responsibilities but also enhances team cohesion and communication proficiency. This proactive approach helps identify potential gaps in knowledge or communication before an actual incident occurs, allowing teams to refine their strategies and become more adept at managing incidents efficiently.

7.3 Post-Incident Analysis and Reporting

Conducting a thorough post-incident analysis is essential for understanding the factors that led to an incident and for preventing future occurrences. The first step is to gather all relevant data, which includes logs, alerts, and eyewitness accounts during the incident. It's vital to create a timeline that captures the sequence of events, helping to clarify how the incident unfolded. Involving a multidisciplinary team during this analysis can further enrich the insights, incorporating views from IT, security, and operational perspectives. This collaborative approach facilitates a fuller understanding of the incident and promotes accountability. It's also crucial to assess the response: was it timely and effective? What protocols were activated, and were any gaps identified in existing procedures? This reflection not only pinpoints shortcomings but also illuminates best practices that worked well.

The significance of reporting and integrating lessons learned into future plans cannot be overstated. Well-documented reports serve as a reference point for similar incidents and help other teams learn from past mistakes. They should cover the incident's nature, the impact it had on the organization, and the effectiveness of the response. Sharing these findings fosters a culture of transparency and continuous improvement within an organization. Additionally, incorporating insights into future planning is vital; this can manifest as updated training programs, revised incident response plans, or even enhancements in technology. Reporting is not merely an exercise in bureaucracy but a strategic function that shapes the organization's resilience against future threats. By documenting lessons learned, professionals can fortify defenses and prepare for evolving cyber threats.

Ultimately, the post-incident analysis and reporting process offers invaluable perspectives that enhance an organization's security posture. Cybersecurity professionals must not only focus on immediate incident management but also on the long-term implications of their findings. Adopting a proactive mindset towards integrating lessons learned ensures that each incident becomes a building block towards a more robust security framework. Consider implementing a regular schedule for reviews of past incidents, enabling ongoing enhancements in strategy, technology, and team readiness.

8. The Role of Encryption in Cyber Security

8.1 Types of Encryption Techniques

Understanding the types of encryption techniques is fundamental for cybersecurity professionals as they form the backbone of data protection strategies. Two primary methods exist: symmetric and asymmetric encryption. Symmetric encryption uses a single key for both encryption and decryption, making it faster and more efficient for processing large volumes of data. The challenge here lies in key distribution; if the key is intercepted, the security of the entire system can be compromised. In contrast, asymmetric encryption, also known as public key cryptography, employs a pair of keys: one public and one private. This method enhances security as the public key can be shared openly while the private key remains confidential. Asymmetric encryption is crucial for establishing secure communications, such as in SSL/TLS protocols, where it ensures that data can be exchanged safely over insecure channels.

Different encryption techniques have specific use cases that highlight their importance in data protection. For organizations, symmetric encryption is effective for securing data at rest, such as files stored on servers or databases. This method is often implemented in scenarios where speed is essential, like encrypting large datasets during processing. On the other hand, asymmetric encryption plays a vital role in secure email communication and digital signatures. By using asymmetric encryption, senders can ensure that only the intended recipient can access sensitive information while also verifying the authenticity of the sender. Combined approaches are also common; for instance, a system may use asymmetric encryption to securely exchange a symmetric key, which then encrypts the actual data. Understanding these use cases is crucial for professionals tasked with safeguarding sensitive information against cyber threats. Continuous evaluation of the encryption methods employed can lead to strengthened security measures, ensuring that data remains protected across various platforms and applications.

Cybersecurity experts should consider the specific requirements of their organization while selecting encryption techniques. Performance, security needs, and the nature of the data being protected are factors that should guide their decisions. Implementing strong key management practices is also essential, as the strength of an encryption method is fundamentally linked to how well the keys are safeguarded. Regularly updating and rotating encryption keys can help mitigate risks associated with key compromise. By staying informed about the latest advancements in encryption technology and adapting strategies accordingly, professionals can enhance their data protection measures significantly.

8.2 Encryption Standards and Protocols

Industry-standard encryption protocols such as AES (Advanced Encryption Standard), RSA (Rivest-Shamir-Adleman), and SSL/TLS (Secure Sockets Layer/Transport Layer Security) play crucial roles in securing data in transit and at rest. AES is a symmetric encryption algorithm that is widely adopted due to its speed and efficiency, making it suitable for encrypting large amounts of data. RSA, on the other hand, is an asymmetric encryption method that uses a pair of keys for encryption and decryption, providing robust security for sensitive data exchange, particularly in scenarios like email and digital signatures. SSL/TLS are essential protocols for establishing secure connections over the internet, ensuring safe communications between clients and servers. By implementing these protocols, organizations can protect sensitive information from prying eyes and malicious attacks.

Understanding the importance of adhering to established encryption standards is vital for cybersecurity professionals. Compliance with these standards not only enhances data security but also builds trust with clients and stakeholders. Organizations that follow industry standards are less likely to suffer from data breaches, as strong encryption helps mitigate risks associated with unauthorized access. Moreover, regulatory frameworks often require the use of certain encryption methods to protect personal and sensitive data. Organizations that neglect these standards may find themselves subject to legal penalties and reputational damage. Therefore, embracing established encryption protocols is a fundamental practice that cybersecurity professionals must prioritize in their security strategies.

It's essential to stay updated with encryption advancements and changes in standards, as the field of cybersecurity is continuously evolving. New vulnerabilities emerge regularly, prompting updates to existing protocols or the establishment of new ones. Cybersecurity professionals should engage in ongoing education and training to ensure they are proficient in the latest encryption standards and understand how to implement them effectively. By doing so, they can better protect their organizations from potential threats and ensure the integrity and confidentiality of sensitive information.

8.3 Best Practices for Implementing Encryption

Effective encryption implementation requires a thorough understanding of an organization's unique operational context and the specific data protection needs that arise from it. Firstly, it is essential to assess the types of data being handled, identifying sensitive information that warrants encryption. This assessment should guide the selection of appropriate encryption methods, such as symmetric or asymmetric encryption, based on performance, security requirements, and regulatory compliance. Additionally, organizations must consider their data encryption strategy throughout its lifecycle, from data at rest to data in transit. Deploying strong key management practices is crucial, as it protects the encryption keys themselves. Strong authentication mechanisms and access controls should be employed to ensure that only authorized personnel can access sensitive information and encryption keys. Regular updates and system maintenance further contribute to a resilient encryption strategy, showcasing the importance of adaptability in a rapidly evolving cyber threat landscape. Empowering teams with training on encryption practices not only boosts compliance but fosters a culture of security awareness within the organization.

Despite the best intentions, many organizations fall into common pitfalls during encryption implementation. One prevalent issue is the over-reliance on encryption as the sole security measure. While encryption is a critical component of a comprehensive security strategy, it should never be seen as a panacea. Organizations often overlook the importance of protecting the entire infrastructure, potentially leaving vulnerabilities exposed. Another significant error is inadequate key management. Poorly managed keys can lead to unauthorized access or data loss, rendering the encryption ineffective. Additionally, failing to keep pace with evolving encryption standards and technologies introduces vulnerabilities. Regularly reviewing and updating encryption protocols is vital to address emerging threats. It's also not uncommon for organizations to neglect user education about encryption, risking improper use or misconfiguration. Therefore, combating these pitfalls requires a balanced approach that integrates encryption with a broader security framework while ensuring staff is adequately trained.

A practical tip for cybersecurity professionals is to establish regular audits of encryption practices. These audits can evaluate the effectiveness of encryption processes, identify areas for improvement, and ensure compliance with evolving regulations. By systematically reviewing encryption protocols, organizations can better adapt to new threats, maintaining a robust security posture while protecting sensitive data.

9. Endpoint Security Strategies

9.1 Importance of Endpoint Security

Securing endpoints is critical in the modern cyber threat landscape. Endpoints—devices such as laptops, smartphones, and tablets—are often the most vulnerable points in a corporate network. With the rise of remote work and bring-your-own-device (BYOD) policies, the number of endpoints has proliferated, creating a larger attack surface for cybercriminals to exploit. Every unsecured endpoint represents a potential breach point, and these devices not only access sensitive data but also can act as gateways for malware and other attacks. As attackers become more sophisticated, the need for comprehensive endpoint security becomes even more essential for safeguarding organizational assets and maintaining customer trust.

The risks associated with unsecured endpoints are numerous and complex. An unprotected device may be an easy target for attackers looking to gain unauthorized access to corporate networks. Once inside, the attackers can move laterally, compromising other connected devices and sensitive data. Additionally, unsecured endpoints can lead to data leaks, which can result in severe financial repercussions and regulatory penalties. Threats such as ransomware can also take advantage of vulnerable endpoints, encrypting data and demanding hefty ransom fees. Outdated software or weak security configurations can increase vulnerabilities, making regular updates and robust security measures paramount to protect against these evolving threats.

Effective endpoint security strategies should involve a multi-layered approach that combines technologies such as antivirus software, firewalls, and intrusion detection systems, along with user education and training. Regular assessments of endpoint vulnerabilities and compliance with security policies are also crucial. As the cyber threat landscape continues to evolve, organizations must remain vigilant and proactive in their endpoint security measures to defend against ever-increasing risks. Implementing a zero-trust framework can further enhance security by treating all endpoints as untrusted until proven otherwise, thereby minimizing potential attack vectors. Investing in advanced endpoint security solutions is not just a technical requirement; it's a crucial aspect of safeguarding an organization's future.

9.2 Endpoint Detection and Response (EDR) Solutions

Endpoint Detection and Response (EDR) solutions have emerged as crucial tools for modern cybersecurity strategies, specifically designed to detect, investigate, and respond to cyber threats targeting endpoint devices. These systems leverage various capabilities, including real-time monitoring, automatic data collection, and advanced analytics to identify suspicious activities. By utilizing behavioural analysis and machine learning algorithms, EDR solutions can accurately differentiate between benign and malevolent activities, effectively reducing the noise of false positives. Threat intelligence further enhances these capabilities, allowing organizations to stay ahead by recognizing known and emerging threats. The proactive nature of EDR not only focuses on detection but also equips security teams with the tools to respond swiftly, containing incidents before they escalate into larger breaches.

Implementing EDR tools significantly enhances an organization's overall security posture. By providing continuous visibility into endpoint activities, these solutions help identify vulnerabilities sooner, allowing organizations to prioritize their responses based on potential impact. EDR systems also facilitate better incident response by enabling security teams to investigate events retrospectively, thereby understanding attacker behaviours and tactics. This knowledge assists in refining defensive strategies and improving threat prevention measures. The integration of EDR with other security solutions, such as Security Information and Event Management (SIEM) systems and threat hunting initiatives, creates a comprehensive security ecosystem that strengthens proactive defenses and reinforces resilience against cyberattacks.

To maximize the effectiveness of EDR solutions, organizations should ensure they have robust processes for incident response and threat intelligence sharing in place. Establishing clear protocols for responding to alerts and incidents can streamline operations and improve response times. Additionally, investing in training your security team on the functionalities of the EDR tool can empower them to utilize its features fully, leading to more effective detection and remediation efforts. Regularly updating and fine-tuning EDR configurations based on evolving threat landscapes is essential for maintaining robust protection.

9.3 Securing Mobile and IoT Devices

Securing mobile devices and IoT endpoints presents unique challenges due to their pervasive nature and diverse functionalities. The vast number of mobile applications, varying operating systems, and different user behaviours contribute to a complex security landscape. Cybersecurity professionals face numerous obstacles, including unpatched vulnerabilities, the risks associated with public Wi-Fi networks, and the increasing sophistication of cyber threats. Moreover, the sheer volume of IoT devices connected to networks often leads to a lack of visibility, making it difficult to monitor and manage vulnerabilities effectively. Strategies to address these challenges should include a robust framework for device authentication and strong access control measures, enabling secure communication between devices and the network. It is also vital to implement regular updates and patches, ensuring that devices are protected against newly discovered threats.

To ensure security across diverse device ecosystems, adopting best practices is essential. Organizations should consider implementing a comprehensive security policy that encompasses all device types and usage scenarios. This includes employing strong encryption methods for data transmission and storage, enforcing multi-factor authentication, and conducting regular security audits to identify and remediate vulnerabilities. Employee training is a critical aspect; users must be educated about the risks associated with mobile and IoT devices, such as phishing attempts and insecure app downloads. Regularly updating firmware and software can significantly reduce the attack surface, while also considering device lifecycle management to phase out outdated technology responsibly. Lastly, integrating security solutions that provide centralized visibility and control can empower organizations to effectively monitor and respond to security incidents across all devices, thus enhancing the overall security posture.

10. Network Security Fundamentals

10.1 Network Segmentation Techniques

Network segmentation is essential in modern cyber defense strategies as it effectively limits attack surfaces by creating barriers between different segments of a network. By isolating sensitive areas of the network, organizations can contain potential breaches and minimize the impact of an attack. This practice not only protects critical systems and data but also enhances visibility into network activity, making it easier to detect anomalies. When a breach occurs in one segment, segmentation helps prevent lateral movement, stopping attackers from accessing other parts of the network. This layered approach to security supports compliance with regulations that require strict access controls and data protection measures.

Implementing effective network segmentation involves adhering to best practices that approach the challenge systematically. Organizations should start by mapping out their entire network, identifying all devices, applications, and data flows to understand the current architecture. This insight allows for informed decision-making about how to create segments based on function, data sensitivity, and access requirements. Limiting access to each segment is a critical step; implementing the principle of least privilege ensures that users and applications have only the necessary rights to perform their tasks. Additionally, organizations should consider using firewalls, intrusion detection systems, and virtual LANs (VLANs) to reinforce segmentation and monitor traffic between segments. Regularly reviewing and updating segmentation strategies based on evolving network conditions and threat landscapes is crucial for maintaining security effectiveness.

For optimal security, it is also beneficial to create a policy framework around segmentation that includes incident response and recovery plans. Such policies should delineate responsibilities, procedures for monitoring segment integrity, and guidelines for adapting to new threats or vulnerabilities. Moreover, integrating segmentation into existing security operations can enhance threat detection capabilities, allowing security teams to react quickly to incidents within each segment. A practical tip for organizations looking to enhance their network security is to conduct regular drills and simulations that test the effectiveness of segmentation policies, ensuring that staff are prepared for real-world scenarios.

10.2 Firewalls and Intrusion Detection Systems

Firewalls and Intrusion Detection Systems (IDS) are fundamental components of modern network security. Firewalls act as a barrier between an internal network and external threats, controlling the incoming and outgoing traffic based on predetermined security rules. They function by examining packets of data and determining whether to allow or block them. While traditional firewalls focus on filtering based on IP addresses and ports, next-generation firewalls also incorporate application awareness and deep packet inspection to enhance security. On the other hand, Intrusion Detection Systems monitor network traffic for suspicious activities and potential threats, alerting administrators when malicious behaviour is detected. Together, these technologies form a multi-layered defense strategy, helping organizations effectively protect sensitive data and maintain the integrity of their networks.

When comparing different types of firewalls, we find several categories, including network-based firewalls, host-based firewalls, and application-layer firewalls. Network-based firewalls are typically deployed at the network's perimeter, attempting to protect an entire network. Host-based firewalls are installed on individual devices and offer a granular approach to security, ideal for securing specific endpoints. Application-layer firewalls, on the other hand, operate at the application level, allowing for more in-depth traffic inspection and control, particularly for web-based applications. Intrusion Detection Systems also come in various forms: network-based IDS monitors traffic as it passes through a network, while host-based IDS monitors individual devices for signs of intrusion. Some IDS solutions also incorporate Intrusion Prevention Systems (IPS), taking proactive measures against detected threats, effectively blocking them before they can cause harm. Understanding these distinctions is crucial for cybersecurity professionals tasked with selecting and implementing the right safeguards for their organization.

In the ever-evolving landscape of cybersecurity threats, it's essential to remember that no single solution can offer complete protection. Firewalls and IDS technologies should be part of a comprehensive security strategy that includes regular updates, patch management, and continuous monitoring. Cybersecurity professionals must stay informed about emerging threats and continuously evaluate their firewall and IDS configurations to adapt to new vulnerabilities and attack vectors. Maintaining an effective incident response plan adds another layer of preparation, allowing organizations to swiftly address security breaches as they occur. This proactive approach not only minimizes potential damage but also reinforces the overall resilience of the network security posture.

10.3 Best Practices for Secure Network Configurations

Establishing secure configurations in network devices is crucial for protecting sensitive data and maintaining the integrity of an organization's IT infrastructure. This begins with the adoption of a baseline configuration that reflects an organization's security policies. One of the primary steps is ensuring that default passwords and settings are changed immediately following device installation. Default settings are well-known and can be exploited by malicious actors, making it imperative to customize every configuration. Additionally, implementing role-based access control ensures that users have only the permissions they require to perform their jobs, mitigating the risk of unauthorized access.

Network segmentation is another vital strategy. By dividing the network into smaller, manageable zones, organizations can limit the spread of threats and better control access to sensitive data. Employing firewalls, intrusion detection systems, and access control lists helps in monitoring and regulating traffic. Regular security auditing and configuration review enhance the integrity of device settings, allowing for timely identification and rectification of any potential misconfigurations. Tools designed for configuration management can automate this process, ensuring that secure standards are not only implemented but also maintained over time.

Misconfigurations can have significant implications on overall security, potentially leading to data breaches, unauthorized access, and significant business downtime. Common misconfigurations include overly permissive access controls, exposed management interfaces, and unpatched software vulnerabilities. Each of these errors can create an avenue for attackers to exploit, thereby jeopardizing the organization's security posture. One often-overlooked issue is the lack of change management processes, which leads to unauthorized or undocumented changes that can introduce vulnerabilities. It's essential to develop a rigorous process that includes documentation of changes, along with an approval process that thoroughly assesses the security implications of alterations before they are applied.

The impact of these misconfigurations can extend beyond immediate risks. They can also erode customer trust, result in regulatory fines, and disrupt business continuity. Regular training and awareness programs for IT staff can improve their understanding of secure configurations and the potential pitfalls of misconfiguration. Establishing a culture of security within the organization fosters mindfulness of security practices at every level. To help mitigate risks associated with misconfigurations, generating regular reports that evaluate device configurations against established security benchmarks can provide insights and accountability, driving continuous improvement in secure network practices.

Ultimately, remaining vigilant about both secure configurations and the implications of misconfigurations will foster a stronger defense against potential threats. Employing a proactive approach to network security that includes routine assessments, updates, and education for all relevant personnel can significantly reduce vulnerabilities. As a practical tip, organizations should integrate automated tools for continuous monitoring and alerts whenever an unauthorized change to network device configurations occurs, which allows for faster remedial actions and a more resilient security infrastructure.

11. Compliance and Regulatory Frameworks

11.1 Overview of Cyber Security Regulations

An in-depth look at various compliance regulations impacting organizations globally reveals that these regulations serve as critical frameworks for businesses operating in an increasingly digital landscape. Key regulations such as the General Data Protection Regulation (GDPR) in the European Union, the Health Insurance Portability and Accountability Act (HIPAA) in the United States, and the Payment Card Industry Data Security Standard (PCI DSS) establish rigorous standards for the collection, storage, and processing of sensitive data. Organizations are often required to implement stringent security measures to protect personal information and ensure that their practices are in line with these regulations. The complexity of navigating these regulations can be daunting, as they vary not only by region but also by industry. Compliance requires continuous monitoring of evolving legal standards, and organizations must establish robust systems to assess and manage risks associated with data handling. The implications of non-compliance can be severe, including hefty fines, reputational damage, and loss of customer trust, all of which underscore the paramount importance of adherence to cybersecurity regulations.

The significance of regulatory compliance in fostering organizational accountability cannot be overstated. Compliance encourages a culture of responsibility within organizations, pushing them to prioritize the protection of sensitive information and implement comprehensive cybersecurity policies. It establishes clear expectations for how organizations should manage data, communicate with stakeholders, and respond to incidents. This accountability not only mitigates risks but also enhances a company's credibility in the marketplace. By aligning with regulatory standards, organizations can demonstrate to their clients and partners that they are serious about safeguarding data integrity and privacy. This builds trust and can be a competitive differentiator in a crowded market. Moreover, regular compliance assessments drive continuous improvement in security practices, enabling organizations to adapt to new threats and challenges in a proactive manner.

Understanding these regulations is essential for cybersecurity professionals tasked with protecting organizational assets. Keeping abreast of legislative changes and their implications can make a significant difference in how effectively organizations handle data security challenges. For those in the field, it is beneficial to develop strategies that not only meet regulatory requirements but also enhance overall security posture. An effective approach includes conducting regular risk assessments, training staff on compliance requirements, and integrating compliance into the overarching security strategy, thus ensuring that regulatory mandates strengthen, rather than hinder, the organization's ability to defend against cyber threats.

11.2 Impact of GDPR, HIPAA, and Other Policies

The General Data Protection Regulation (GDPR) and the Health Insurance Portability and Accountability Act (HIPAA) serve as foundational frameworks that significantly influence how organizations manage data privacy and security. GDPR, implemented in 2018 across the European Union, sets rigorous standards for data protection, emphasizing the rights of individuals to control their personal information. It mandates that organizations implement measures that ensure data minimization, transparency, and accountability. Compliance with GDPR requires organizations to adopt a proactive approach to data management, including conducting data protection impact assessments and ensuring comprehensive documentation of data processing activities. For non-compliance, organizations face steep fines, which can reach up to 4% of annual global revenue or €20 million, whichever is greater. On the other hand, HIPAA provides essential guidelines specifically for healthcare entities, ensuring the protection of sensitive patient information. It emphasizes the confidentiality, integrity, and availability of health data, requiring appropriate administrative, physical, and technical safeguards. Organizations must implement strong access controls, conduct regular audits, and ensure that all employees are adequately trained in confidentiality requirements. The implications of these regulations not only shape organizational practices but also affect how cybersecurity professionals design and implement their security architectures.

Beyond GDPR and HIPAA, other policies play a crucial role in shaping cybersecurity practices within organizations. For instance, the California Consumer Privacy Act (CCPA) enhances privacy rights and consumer protection for residents of California, offering more autonomy over personal data collected by businesses. It compels organizations to disclose information on data collection and provides consumers with the right to opt-out of the sale of their personal data. Several other sector-specific regulations, such as the Payment Card Industry Data Security Standard (PCI DSS), impose stringent data security requirements on organizations handling credit card information. These policies create a multifaceted regulatory environment that demands cybersecurity professionals to stay informed and agile. Incorporating these frameworks into everyday cybersecurity practices means ensuring that security measures align not only with legal requirements but also with the evolving landscape of data threats. Employees must be trained not only on the technical aspects of security but also on the regulatory context of the data they handle.

Understanding the implications of GDPR, HIPAA, and other relevant policies is essential for cybersecurity professionals looking to navigate this complex landscape. Organizations are encouraged to integrate compliance into their broader risk management strategies. This involves fostering a culture of compliance, where all employees recognize the importance of adhering to data policies, and where regular training and awareness programs are prioritized. Leveraging technology, such as automated compliance tools, can simplify the monitoring and reporting of compliance metrics, helping organizations to stay ahead of regulatory requirements. The key to thriving in a heavily regulated environment lies in creating secure, transparent, and resilient data practices that not only protect sensitive information but also build trust with stakeholders.

11.3 Navigating Compliance Challenges

Organizations today encounter a myriad of challenges while striving to stay compliant with various regulations. One significant hurdle is the rapid pace of regulatory changes. As laws evolve, cybersecurity professionals must ensure that their policies and systems are updated accordingly to meet new standards. Additionally, the complexity of regulations can lead to confusion about what is required, particularly when businesses operate across multiple jurisdictions, each with its own compliance requirements. The challenge is further compounded by limited resources; many organizations struggle to allocate sufficient time and personnel to compliance efforts without detracting from their core responsibilities. Furthermore, the integration of new technologies can create additional compliance demands. Cloud services, artificial intelligence, and machine learning introduce novel risks and require adherence to stringent regulations, making it vital for security teams to stay informed and proactive.

Overcoming compliance obstacles while maintaining security demands a strategic approach. First, maintaining a thorough understanding of applicable regulations is essential. This can be achieved by conducting regular compliance audits and leveraging compliance management tools that offer real-time insights into regulatory obligations. Adopting a risk-based approach allows organizations to prioritize compliance efforts based on potential risks, thereby optimizing resource allocation and enhancing security measures. It is crucial to foster a culture of compliance across the organization, ensuring employees at all levels recognize their roles in adhering to regulations. Ongoing training programs can empower staff with knowledge about compliance requirements and best practices, reinforcing a collective commitment to security. Collaborating with legal experts and compliance specialists can also provide invaluable guidance, ensuring that organizations navigate complexities with confidence and clarity. By integrating compliance efforts into the overall cybersecurity strategy, organizations can not only meet regulatory demands but also enhance their security posture, ultimately protecting their data and reputation.

For cybersecurity professionals, staying abreast of the regulatory landscape and understanding the implications of compliance on security is paramount. Developing a comprehensive compliance framework that aligns with business objectives can enable organizations to proactively address compliance challenges while safeguarding their networks and systems. Regularly reviewing and updating compliance strategies will not only ensure adherence to regulations but also build trust with stakeholders, customers, and partners. In the ever-evolving world of cybersecurity, this proactive stance toward compliance can become a competitive advantage, fostering resilience in the face of regulatory uncertainties.

12. The Human Element in Cyber Security

12.1 Social Engineering and Human Behaviour

Social engineering is a method used by malicious actors to manipulate individuals into divulging confidential information or performing actions that compromise security. This tactic is heavily reliant on an understanding of human psychology, as attackers leverage emotional responses and cognitive biases to achieve their goals. By exploiting basic human instincts, such as trust, fear, or the desire for social acceptance, perpetrators can craft believable scenarios that appear legitimate. For instance, they often impersonate trusted figures, like company executives or IT personnel, making it easier for them to gain access to sensitive data. This manipulation hinges on the ability to create a false sense of urgency or provide rewards that spur the target into action without critically evaluating the risks involved.

Examining real-world cases reveals how effective these strategies can be. One notable incident involved a cybercriminal posing as a company's system administrator, calling employees to inform them about a supposed security breach. Utilizing authoritative language and a pressure-inducing tone, they coerced several staff members into providing their login credentials. This attack not only compromised the organization's network but also highlighted how individuals, often considered the weakest link in cybersecurity, can inadvertently facilitate breaches simply through trust. Another case involved an attacker who sent phishing emails that mimicked internal communications about a software upgrade. The emails prompted employees to enter their usernames and passwords on a fake website, resulting in stolen credentials that provided unfettered access to sensitive company information.

Reflecting on these case studies emphasizes that while technological defenses are vital, the human element remains a critical consideration in cybersecurity strategies. Training employees to recognize social engineering tactics, such as suspicious calls or emails, can significantly reduce the likelihood of successful attacks. Organizations should routinely conduct awareness programs that highlight the psychological principles at play in social engineering schemes. By fostering a culture of vigilance and encouraging staff to question unexpected requests for information, companies can greatly fortify their defenses against such deceptive practices.

Promoting a proactive attitude towards recognizing social engineering attempts is essential for enhancing overall security. Regularly testing employees through simulated phishing exercises can help reinforce this awareness and gauge the effectiveness of training programs.

12.2 Training and Awareness Programs

Training programs are essential in the realm of cybersecurity because a significant portion of breaches occurs due to human error. By providing comprehensive training, organizations can empower their employees to recognize potential threats and respond appropriately. Employees who are aware of security practices are less likely to fall victim to phishing attacks, inadvertently expose sensitive information, or engage in risky behaviours that jeopardize the organization's security posture. Investing in robust training initiatives not only enhances employee knowledge but also cultivates a security-first culture within the organization, allowing all staff members to contribute to protecting the system from internal and external threats.

Creating effective awareness training initiatives requires careful planning and execution. Programs should be tailored to the specific needs and contexts of the organization, considering the unique threats and vulnerabilities it faces. An engaging curriculum that includes real-world scenarios and interactive elements can greatly enhance learning retention. Training should not be a one-time event; rather, it should be ongoing, adapting to the evolving landscape of cyber threats. Regular updates and refresher courses will help keep employees informed about the latest tactics used by cybercriminals, ensuring that awareness remains high. Moreover, fostering an environment where employees feel comfortable reporting potential security issues without fear of repercussions is crucial for building a dependable defense against cyberattacks.

Monitoring and measuring the effectiveness of these programs through assessments and feedback can provide valuable insights into gaps in knowledge and areas for improvement. Organizations should implement metrics to gauge the success of their training initiatives, such as tracking the reduction in successful phishing attempts over time or analyzing employee engagement rates in training modules. This data can guide future training efforts and highlight the importance of continuous learning in a cyberspace that is constantly evolving. Lastly, the integration of gamification elements can enhance the engagement level of training programs, making learning fun and motivating while simultaneously reinforcing critical cybersecurity concepts.

12.3 The Role of Leadership in Cyber Hygiene

Leadership plays a critical role in establishing a cyber-safe culture within an organization. Cultivating an environment where cyber hygiene is prioritized begins at the top, as leaders set the tone for the behaviour and attitudes of their teams. When executives visibly commit to cybersecurity initiatives, they not only influence the organization's policies and practices but also encourage employees to adopt their own cyber hygiene practices. A leader's emphasis on cybersecurity can transform it from a mere technical concern into a core principle of the organization's culture. This proactive engagement fosters an atmosphere where every employee feels responsible for maintaining robust cyber hygiene, as they recognize that cybersecurity is everyone's role, not just that of the IT department.

Leaders can implement various strategies to foster an environment with strong cyber hygiene. First, providing ongoing education and training helps equip employees with the knowledge they need to recognize threats such as phishing attacks and social engineering schemes. Regular workshops or e-learning modules that cover current cyber risks reinforce a culture of awareness and vigilance. Additionally, leaders can encourage open communication regarding cybersecurity incidents or near-misses, allowing the organization to learn from mistakes and improve practices. Establishing clear policies regarding acceptable use of technology and data management is also essential, as is the implementation of tools that enable secure collaboration while minimizing risks. By rewarding positive behaviour—such as reporting potential security threats—leaders can further strengthen the commitment to cyber hygiene within their teams.

Focusing on these aspects, leadership can create a resilient organizational culture where cybersecurity is integrated into everyday practices. It is important for leaders to regularly assess and adjust their strategies based on evolving threats and organizational changes. By doing so, they ensure that their teams remain not just compliant but actively engaged in the mission of protecting the organization from cyber threats. Establishing a cyber hygiene culture is not a one-time effort but rather an ongoing journey that requires persistent attention and dedication from leadership at all levels.

13. Cyber Security Tools and Technologies

13.1 Overview of Key Security Tools

Essential security tools form the backbone of an effective cybersecurity strategy. In today's digital world, these tools help organizations protect their networks and sensitive data against a growing array of cyber threats. Firewall systems act as gatekeepers, controlling incoming and outgoing traffic based on predetermined security rules. Intrusion detection systems (IDS) and intrusion prevention systems (IPS) further bolster defenses by monitoring network activities for suspicious behaviour and taking action to mitigate potential threats. Endpoint protection software safeguards individual devices, ensuring that laptops, servers, and mobile devices are secure from malware and data breaches.

These tools address various cybersecurity needs by providing layered defenses. For example, security information and event management (SIEM) solutions aggregate and analyze data from multiple sources, helping security teams detect and respond to threats in real time. Vulnerability scanners identify weaknesses in systems and applications, allowing organizations to remediate issues before they can be exploited. Additionally, data encryption tools ensure that sensitive information remains protected both at rest and in transit. Effective incident response tools enable teams to act swiftly during security breaches, minimizing damage and restoring normal operations. By implementing a combination of these tools, organizations can create a robust security posture that adapts to evolving threats and compliance requirements.

Regularly updating and maintaining these security tools is crucial for ongoing effectiveness. Cyber threats continuously evolve, and so must the strategies employed to counter them. Training staff on the proper use of these tools enhances their effectiveness and promotes a security-first culture within the organization. Emphasizing the importance of threat awareness and quick response can significantly improve an organization's resilience against cyber attacks, making the implementation and integration of these essential tools not just beneficial but necessary.

13.2 Evaluating Security Technologies

Assessment criteria for evaluating cybersecurity technologies are essential to ensure that organizations invest in solutions that truly meet their security needs. It's important to begin by identifying the specific risks and vulnerabilities that the organization faces. Understanding the context in which a technology will be deployed helps in evaluating its relevance and effectiveness. Performance metrics should be closely analyzed, including real-time response capabilities, scalability, and ease of integration with existing systems. Additionally, factors such as the technology's ability to comply with regulatory requirements and industry standards should be considered. Evaluators should also assess the total cost of ownership, including initial acquisition costs and ongoing operational expenses. Another crucial aspect is the vendor's reputation and their history of promptly addressing vulnerabilities and providing updates. The user experience is also important; a technology that is difficult to use can lead to decreased adoption and increase the likelihood of human error, undermining security efforts.

Insights into vendor selection and technology procurement processes can significantly impact the effectiveness of cybersecurity measures. The evaluation process should begin with thorough research on potential vendors and their offerings. Consider engaging with multiple vendors to get a comprehensive view of the solutions available. This can aid in comparing features, pricing, and support services. Implementing demonstration periods or pilot tests provides practical insights into how a solution performs under real conditions. It also allows for gathering feedback from the end-users who will be interacting with the technology daily. Emphasizing strong relationship building with vendors can lead to better support and potential customization of solutions. Moreover, it is wise to take into account the vendor's commitment to innovation and their roadmap for future developments, as cybersecurity is an ever-evolving field. Establishing clear communication and expectations during the procurement process ensures alignment of goals and fosters a partnership that can evolve as the organization's needs change.

One practical tip in evaluating security technologies is to prioritize continuous learning and adaptation. Regularly reassess the organization's security landscape and be willing to pivot in response to emerging threats or changes in technology. Establishing a framework for ongoing training and knowledge sharing among staff can enhance the effectiveness of any chosen security technology and create a culture of vigilance within the organization.

13.3 Future Trends in Cyber Security Technologies

Emerging technologies are redefining the landscape of cybersecurity, shaping how organizations protect their digital assets. Artificial intelligence (AI) and machine learning (ML) are at the forefront of these advancements, enabling systems to detect threats in real time by analyzing vast amounts of data more efficiently than human analysts. These technologies can learn from patterns and adapt their responses, offering a proactive defense mechanism against increasingly sophisticated cyber threats. In addition to AI and ML, the integration of advanced analytics and behavioural biometrics provides a multi-layered security approach. These tools not only monitor user behaviours to identify anomalies but also continuously enhance learning algorithms, creating a persistent state of vigilance against potential breaches. Blockchain technology is also gaining traction in cybersecurity, especially for secure data sharing and establishing trust among parties in various transactions. The decentralized nature of blockchain minimizes risks associated with data integrity and unauthorized access, making it an attractive solution for organizations that prioritize security.

Looking ahead, the evolution and integration of these new security technologies will likely lead to a more holistic approach to cybersecurity. Predictive analytics will play a crucial role, as organizations increasingly rely on historical data to forecast potential vulnerabilities. Future cybersecurity systems will likely feature enhanced automation capabilities, streamlining threat response processes while allowing security professionals to focus on strategic initiatives rather than routine tasks. The integration of Internet of Things (IoT) devices will also influence cybersecurity, necessitating more robust security protocols as more devices connect to networks. This interconnectedness will demand a shift towards zero-trust architectures, which assume that threats could exist both outside and inside the network perimeter. Consequently, continuous verification of users and devices will become critical. Furthermore, the growing emphasis on privacy-aware solutions will promote technologies that empower users, giving them greater control over their personal information while ensuring compliance with regulatory frameworks.

As cyber threats evolve, staying ahead requires a commitment to ongoing education and adaptation. Cybersecurity professionals should invest time in understanding new technologies and best practices, including threat intelligence sharing to benefit from collective knowledge. Establishing a culture of security awareness within organizations is equally essential, as human error remains a significant factor in many breaches. Organizations must prioritize ongoing training and resources to equip employees with the knowledge they need to recognize and mitigate risks effectively. Keeping abreast of developments in cybersecurity technologies will empower professionals to make informed decisions that bolster their organization's resilience against future threats.

14. Future of Cyber Threats and Cyber Security

14.1 Emerging Threat Vectors

Identification of new and evolving threat vectors in the cybersecurity landscape has become increasingly critical as technology advances and organizations embrace more complex digital environments. Factors such as the proliferation of the Internet of Things (IoT), the growing reliance on cloud services, and the shift to remote work have all contributed to a dynamic threat landscape. Cybercriminals continuously exploit vulnerabilities in these technologies, often leveraging sophisticated methods such as artificial intelligence to craft more effective attacks. The rise of supply chain attacks, where threat actors infiltrate organizations through third-party vendors, further complicates the situation. Additionally, social engineering tactics have evolved, with attackers using personalized information gathered from social media and other online platforms to manipulate individuals into revealing sensitive data. Understanding these new vectors is essential for cybersecurity professionals tasked with protecting their organizations.

The analysis of how these vectors pose challenges for organizations reveals significant hurdles in maintaining robust security postures. Traditional cybersecurity measures often fall short against the evolving tactics of cybercriminals. For instance, many organizations still rely on perimeter defenses, which are inadequate when dealing with insider threats or attacks that bypass the network altogether. Furthermore, the integration of multiple platforms and devices creates numerous entry points for attackers, making it challenging to establish comprehensive visibility and control. Organizations are also faced with the difficulty of keeping their workforce educated and vigilant against ever-changing phishing schemes and social engineering attacks, which often compromise even the most secure systems. The complexity of regulatory compliance further complicates the security landscape, as organizations must adapt to new laws and standards while ensuring their systems remain resilient against sophisticated threats.

To navigate these challenges successfully, organizations should adopt a proactive approach to cybersecurity that emphasizes adaptability and continuous improvement. Implementing a zero-trust architecture, which assumes that threats could be internal, allows organizations to enhance their defense mechanisms significantly. Regular training and simulated attacks can prepare employees to recognize and manage potential threats effectively. Organizations should also invest in threat intelligence to gain insights into the tactics, techniques, and procedures used by cyber adversaries, aiding in the anticipation and mitigation of attacks. By fostering a culture of security awareness and agility, organizations can better protect themselves against emerging threat vectors.

14.2 The Impact of AI and Machine Learning

Artificial Intelligence (AI) and machine learning have emerged as powerful tools in the realm of cybersecurity. Their dual role is particularly significant; on one hand, they enhance security measures and on the other, they can also be exploited to facilitate cyber threats. AI's capabilities allow for real-time anomaly detection, significantly speeding up the identification of suspicious activities. By analyzing vast amounts of data, machine learning algorithms can discern patterns that may elude human analysts. This proactive capacity helps organizations defend against breaches before they escalate into crises. However, cybercriminals also harness these same technologies to develop sophisticated attack strategies. Automated exploits can learn from previous experiences, enabling attackers to refine their methods and evade traditional security measures. The arms race between cybersecurity defense mechanisms and malicious AI tools presents a complex landscape for security professionals to navigate.

Looking towards the future, AI and machine learning will continue to shape cybersecurity strategies. The integration of these technologies will likely lead to more adaptive and resilient security frameworks that can predict and respond to threats in real time. Organizations will need to invest in advanced machine learning systems that can self-improve as they process new data. This evolution will not only enhance threat detection but also facilitate a more intelligent response to incidents. Moreover, as AI technologies advance, ethical considerations surrounding their use in cybersecurity will become increasingly important. It's essential for professionals to stay informed about regulatory developments and best practices to ensure that AI enhances security without infringing on privacy or ethical boundaries. Embracing these innovations can help professionals ahead of attackers while ensuring compliance with evolving legal standards.

As AI continues to transform cybersecurity, professionals must prioritize continuous education in this rapidly changing field. Understanding the capabilities and limitations of AI tools, as well as the potential risks they introduce, will be crucial. Engaging in collaborative partnerships and information sharing within the cybersecurity community can provide valuable insights and strategies for leveraging AI effectively while mitigating its risks. Organizations should consider regular training and simulation exercises that incorporate AI tools to cultivate a workforce adept at countering the next generation of cyber threats.

14.3 Preparing for Future Cyber Security Challenges

To effectively anticipate and respond to upcoming cyber challenges, organizations must implement proactive strategies that extend beyond reactive measures. This involves a thorough risk assessment that identifies potential vulnerabilities in their systems, processes, and employee behaviours. By adopting threat intelligence tools, cybersecurity professionals can gain insights into emerging threats and trends, allowing them to develop informed defenses ahead of time. Collaboration is also essential; sharing information with other organizations within the industry can create a broader understanding of the threat landscape and enhance overall readiness. Conducting regular tabletop exercises and simulations helps organizations gauge their incident response capabilities and refine their strategies, ensuring they are prepared for various scenarios that could arise in the future.

The importance of continuous learning and adaptation in cybersecurity practices cannot be overstated. Cyber threats evolve daily, and staying ahead of these attacks requires a commitment to ongoing education. Professionals should seek opportunities for training and certification in new technologies and methodologies to enhance their skills. Embracing a culture of learning not only strengthens the capabilities of individual team members but also cultivates an organization-wide mindset of agility and innovation. Additionally, monitoring the latest developments in cybersecurity laws, regulations, and ethical standards is crucial, as compliance can significantly impact an organization's risk management framework. Establishing partnerships with educational institutions can facilitate access to research and development in cybersecurity, pushing professionals to stay informed and prepared.

A valuable tip for cybersecurity professionals is to foster a community of practice within their organization. Creating an environment where team members feel encouraged to share experiences, insights, and ongoing education transforms individual efforts into a collective strength. This not only enhances the team's capability to respond to new threats but also builds a more resilient security posture that evolves alongside the threat landscape.

15. Case Studies and Lessons Learned

15.1 Analysis of Major APT Incidents

High-profile advanced persistent threat (APT) incidents have consistently underscored the vulnerabilities faced by organizations across various sectors. These events typically involve long-term, targeted attacks that seek to infiltrate networks and extract sensitive information over an extended period. For instance, the 2015 breach of the U.S. Office of Personnel Management, attributed to APT groups linked to foreign governments, resulted in the theft of personal data from millions of federal employees. The ramifications of this incident went beyond immediate financial loss; they compromised national security and raised questions about the government's ability to safeguard sensitive information. Analyzing such incidents reveals patterns in attackers' methodologies, often rooted in social engineering and zero-day vulnerabilities, which organizations must understand to bolster their defenses.

Lessons derived from these incidents highlight the importance of a proactive security posture to enhance organizational resilience. It is critical for organizations to adopt a multi-layered security strategy that combines robust technical controls with employee training and awareness programs. For instance, investing in threat intelligence and maintaining an updated inventory of assets can drastically reduce the attack surface. Furthermore, organizations should conduct regular penetration testing and simulate attack scenarios to evaluate their response capabilities. This approach not only prepares teams for potential incidents but also fosters a culture of security awareness that permeates the entire organization. Establishing an incident response plan that is regularly updated and tested can greatly improve an organization's ability to react swiftly and effectively when faced with an APT attack.

The ability to share information about previous incidents with peers and industry stakeholders is also crucial. Collaborative efforts can help organizations stay ahead of potential threats by understanding tactics, techniques, and procedures used by attackers. By studying past APT incidents and implementing best practices learned from them, organizations can better prepare for future challenges. Ultimately, fostering a mindset of continuous improvement in cybersecurity practices will be a vital asset in the ongoing battle against APTs. Always ensure that your incident response plan includes a post-incident review process, as this is essential in identifying gaps and areas for enhancement in your security posture.

15.2 Key Takeaways from Successful Cyber Defense

Successful defenses against Advanced Persistent Threats (APTs) often leverage a combination of proactive and reactive strategies tailored to each organization's unique landscape. Organizations that have effectively thwarted APTs emphasize the importance of threat intelligence gathering. These defenses typically start with continuous monitoring for anomalies in network traffic and endpoints. Notable strategies include adopting a zero trust security model, which requires verification for every device and user attempting to access resources, thus minimizing potential risks. Moreover, implementing comprehensive employee training programs fosters a culture of security awareness, enabling team members to identify and respond to potential threats before they escalate. Regularly scheduled penetration tests and red team exercises also serve as critical components. They help organizations identify vulnerabilities and prepare their defenses against real-world attack scenarios.

When it comes to responding during an attack, effective procedures must be in place, focusing on swift containment and eradication of the threat while maintaining business continuity. Clear incident response plans can significantly shorten recovery times and mitigate damages. Establishing a communication protocol ensures that key stakeholders are informed and that there is clarity within the response team regarding their roles. Employing automated incident detection and response tools can enhance the speed of reaction, minimizing the window of opportunity for attackers. Once the threat is neutralized, a thorough post-incident analysis helps in refining existing strategies and bolstering defenses against future APT attempts. This continual cycle of learning and adaptation is crucial for maintaining resilience in the face of evolving threats.

Understanding these key takeaways can significantly boost an organization's cyber defense posture. Prioritizing threat intelligence, ensuring robust incident response plans, and incorporating post-incident reviews can transform how an organization responds to cyber threats. Cyber security professionals must foster an environment where learning from past incidents informs future best practices, thereby enhancing overall preparedness. Focusing on the integration of advanced technologies, human insights, and a culture of vigilance can position organizations favourably against the ever-evolving tactics of cyber adversaries.

15.3 Common Pitfalls in Cyber Security Strategy

Organizations often stumble into a range of common errors when developing their cybersecurity strategies. One major mistake is underestimating the importance of employee training and awareness. Employees can become the weakest link in an organization's defenses if they are not adequately educated about phishing attacks, social engineering tactics, and other cyber threats. Another frequent error is failing to regularly update and patch systems and software. Cyber threats continually evolve, and outdated systems can present easy opportunities for attackers. Many organizations also neglect to conduct regular audits and penetration testing to identify vulnerabilities within their infrastructure. This creates a false sense of security and can lead to disastrous consequences. Lastly, there is often a lack of a comprehensive incident response plan. Without a clear protocol for responding to breaches, organizations may react poorly, exacerbating the damage of an already critical situation.

To avoid these pitfalls and strengthen defenses, organizations should prioritize comprehensive training programs to educate employees about cybersecurity risks and best practices. Regular updates and patches should be integrated into a systematic maintenance routine, ensuring systems are up-to-date and resilient against new threats. Conducting regular audits and penetration tests will help uncover vulnerabilities that might otherwise go unnoticed, allowing organizations to address them proactively. Developing a well-documented incident response plan is crucial, as it should outline roles, responsibilities, and steps to take in the event of a cyber incident. Finally, fostering a culture of accountability and vigilance can go a long way in minimizing risk. By combining awareness with strong protocols and regular assessments, organizations can create a robust cybersecurity framework capable of withstanding the ever-evolving landscape of cyber threats.

An invaluable practical tip is to implement a layered security approach, often referred to as "defense in depth." This strategy involves using multiple security measures across various levels of the IT environment, helping to ensure that if one measure fails, others are still in place to provide protection. This not only enhances overall security but can also reduce the impact of a potential breach.